@RosenTeenTalk

SELF-HARM AND CUTTING

Xina M. Uhl

ROSEN
PUBLISHING

Published in 2024 by The Rosen Publishing Group, Inc.
2544 Clinton Street, Buffalo, NY 14224

First Edition

Editor: Greg Roza
Designer: Rachel Rising

Library of Congress Cataloging-in-Publication Data

Names: Uhl, Xina M., author.
Title: Self-harm and cutting / Xina M. Uhl.
Description: Buffalo : Rosen Publishing, [2024] | Series: @RosenTeenTalk |
   Includes bibliographical references and index.
Identifiers: LCCN 2023009474 (print) | LCCN 2023009475 (ebook) | ISBN
   9781499469370 (library binding) | ISBN 9781499469363 (paperback) | ISBN
   9781499469387 (ebook)
Subjects: LCSH: Cutting (Self-mutilation)--Juvenile literature. |
   Self-mutilation--Juvenile literature.
Classification: LCC RJ506.S44 U35 2024 (print) | LCC RJ506.S44 (ebook) |
   DDC 616.85/8200835--dc23/eng/20230417
LC record available at https://lccn.loc.gov/2023009474
LC ebook record available at https://lccn.loc.gov/2023009475

Manufactured in the United States of America

CPSIA Compliance Information: Batch #CSRYA24. For Further Information contact Rosen Publishing at 1-800-237-9932.

Find us on

CONTENTS

Chapter 1

How It Begins . . .

My mom married Rob just a year after my dad had died. At first, he was nice, but soon he began yelling at my little sister and me all the time. My mom ignored it. One day he came to pick me up after school. As I got in his truck, I moved the tools in the seat so I could sit down. A saw blade scratched my arm, and blood pooled.

Later, when I was alone, I picked at the scratch, and it began to bleed again. I was proud that I could take the pain. I felt like I had power. Using a knife, a nail, and thumb tacks, I began to cut my forearms regularly. I hid the cuts because I felt **ashamed**.

Being a teenager is hard enough without **conflicts** with parents. Some adults don't know how to handle conflicts respectfully.

WHAT IS SELF-HARM?

When a person hurts themselves on purpose, it is self-harm. Some people find **relief** from **anxiety** when they cause pain to their bodies. Others find calm from racing thoughts, or stop feeling hopeless or angry. Some people who self-harm might be suicidal, or in danger of killing themselves. But studies show that most are not. However, self-harm can lead to suicide. It is important that anyone with thoughts of suicide call or text the 24/7 National Suicide Prevention Lifeline at 988.

Doctors have special terms for self-harm. One term is **deliberate** self-harm (DSH). Another is non-suicidal self-injury (NSSI). An injury is harm or damage. They identify symptoms, or signs, such as:

- Hiding wounds, or cuts, under clothing
- Having **injuries** that can't be explained
- Feeling hopeless or worthless
- Avoiding others and staying alone
- Keeping items such as blades, broken glass, and knives where they do not belong

Cutting is the most common form of self-harm.

FORMS OF SELF-HARM

- Cutting yourself with a sharp object
- Hitting yourself or things (like a wall)
- Burning yourself
- Pulling your hair
- Bruising yourself
- Biting yourself
- Breaking bones
- **Piercing** your skin with needles

WHO HARMS THEMSELVES, AND WHY?

Anyone can harm themselves, at any age. This means men, women, **LGBTQ** people, parents, grandparents, teens, and younger children. Some people cut themselves once, and never do it again. Others start cutting when they are pre-teens and continue for many years. It doesn't matter if you are Black, white, American Indian, rich, poor, or in between: Anyone can self-harm.

Studies show that some people have more risk factors than others. Yet there are people with these risk factors who never self-harm. And there are those without risk factors who DO self-harm.

Deadly Activity?

Are people who cut themselves trying to take their own lives? There's no easy answer. Many times they are not. Other times, self-harm may be a "dry run" for a later attempt. That's why **treatment** is so important.

What Is Scarification?

Many Native cultures have **rituals** involving scarring. They cut into the skin to create designs, or patterns. These designs may be rites of passage. Rites of passage honor when people move from one part of their lives to another. For example, graduation is a rite showing that school is over. Ritual scarification can still lead to problems, such as infection, or illness caused by germs.

Can you pick out someone who self-harms from this picture? The answer is no. While some populations are more at risk than others, no one knows for sure who will end up harming themselves.

RISK FACTORS

- Age (teenagers)
- Gender (women)
- Having friends who self-harm
- Using drugs or **alcohol** often
- Having low **self-esteem**
- Feeling **depressed** or anxious

- Having other mental illnesses (illnesses of the mind)
- Suffering from physical (bodily) abuse, or treatment that's harmful or harsh
- Suffering from sexual abuse
- Dealing with family problems such as divorce

GETTING REAL

When asked why people self-harm, they give many reasons. It may give them a sense of relief. It may allow them to cope, or deal with, a problem. Some may cut to stop feeling **numb**, or to **express** feelings of anger or sadness. Other reasons include:

- To lower anxiety
- To block bad memories
- To show a need for help
- To express distress, or suffering
- To **punish** oneself
- To hurt oneself instead of others

Usually, self-harm comes down to two problems. One is an inability to find healthy ways to deal with **emotional** pain. Another is difficulty in controlling emotions. Feelings can combine to trigger, or cause, self-harm, but it can be hard to identify them. Often, people feel worthless. They may feel hopeless too. But the truth is that feelings are not facts.

It is possible to find relief without hurting yourself. You can learn other ways of dealing with pain and expressing your feelings. Many people have overcome the activity of self-harm.

There are people who care about the suffering of others. Some are friends and family, while others are doctors and counselors. A counselor is a person trained in giving guidance to help people deal with problems and achieve goals.

A TRUE FRIEND

My friend Karma texted me one afternoon: *i want to cut myself.*

My heart jumped into my throat. *No,* I sent back, *we'll get thru this together. pinky swear.*

We called a counselor together, and I drove her to the first meeting. Afterward, she said, "I hate him." So we found a different counselor she liked better. It took a while, and a lot of tears. A doctor told her to take medication (drugs) that helped her feel better. One day—the best day in months—she smiled again.

I helped Karma because my friend Sushmita had helped me when I was cutting. I realized being a friend to someone who needs it can be a gift for the helper too.

Chapter 2

TRAITS THAT LEAD TO SELF-HARM

We're all born with positive (good) and negative (bad) **traits**. Some traits, such as being friendly and listening to others, help us get through life. Other traits may cause us to struggle with self-harm, such as often being negative and not very agreeable with others. But traits such as pushing anger deep inside or feeling powerless are not so easy to see. Studies tell us that other self-harming traits include:

- Being unable to take **rejection**
- Being irritable (easily bothered or angered)
- Acting without thinking first
- Ongoing anxiety
- Not making plans
- Feeling unable to cope
- Having **aggressive** feelings, which are directed inward
- Thinking you don't have control over life

If you have one or more of these traits, don't panic. There is hope. We all have one friend who stays with us our whole lives: our thoughts. Our thoughts often shape our actions—for good or bad. We can learn to control our thoughts, though it isn't always easy.

It's easier for some of us to show anger than for others. But we can all learn healthy ways to share our feelings.

CELEBRITIES WHO SELF-HARM

Some celebrities struggle with self-harm too. American actress, songwriter, and singer Demi Lovato has been open about her mental health struggles as a teen. She says, "There were times I felt so anxious, almost like I was crawling out of my skin—that if I didn't do something physical to match the way I felt inside, I would explode . . . I cut myself to take my mind off that. I just didn't care what happened. I had no fear."

Doctors diagnosed her with **bipolar disorder** and an eating disorder. She deals with it by:

- Meditating, or spending time in quiet thought
- Making time to care for herself
- Not reaching for her phone when alone

Pop music star Demi Lovato's songs regularly top the Billboard Music charts. She deals with **substance abuse**, mental health problems, and self-harm.

A FAMOUS STORY

Russell Brand is an actor, comedian, and podcaster. When he was younger, he self-harmed due to anger, **frustration**, and a need to express himself. Now, he attends support groups. There, people talk about their problems. He says, "I find . . . being heard by others really, really helps me. Makes me feel not alone. Makes me feel less weird."

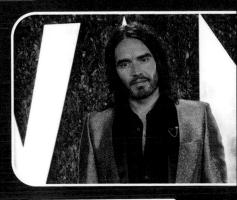

CHILDHOOD ABUSE AND NEGLECT

Children who are mistreated are abused. This abuse can be physical. That means they are hit, shaken, smacked, or kicked. Emotional abuse happens too. This is when a child is put down and called names. It can also be when a child is ignored, rejected, or made to feel worthless.

Sexual abuse can also happen. This means improper touching or **intercourse**. It can also mean:

- Showing children pictures or movies of people having sex
- Taking pictures or videos of children wearing few or no clothes
- Making children act in a sexual way

Studies show that many people who self-harm were abused or neglected as children. People may hurt themselves to gain control over their lives—control they didn't have as children. Others may self-harm because they feel they deserve to be punished.

Children who are abused while young often have serious problems when they grow up.

WHAT IS CHILD NEGLECT?

Neglect means not caring for a child properly. This can mean not giving a child:

- Food
- Clothing
- Affection (showing love and caring for someone)

- Education
- Health care
- A safe and clean home

SUBSTANCE ABUSE

Substance abuse takes many forms. It can be drinking alcohol too much or too often. It can mean popping **fentanyl** pills and smoking **methamphetamine**, or meth. For some, drug and alcohol abuse happens every now and then. For others, it quickly becomes an addiction that must be fed constantly.

Substance abuse often starts in the teen years. It is common among people who live with mental illness. Those who self-harm often abuse drugs and alcohol. Once the drugs wear off, users can feel hopeless and depressed. In this state, they can harm themselves. Self-harm can also cause a desire, or want, to use drugs or alcohol. This creates a circle of abuse that is hard to stop.

Substance abuse takes different forms. One thing is the same, though. Drugs and alcohol change how people feel and act.

WHAT ARE STIMULANTS?

Stimulants are drugs that cause someone to feel more active than usual. Caffeine, something found in coffee, tea, and soft drinks, is a very common stimulant. Others are illegal, or you must have a doctor prescribe them, or order them for you. These include cocaine, methamphetamine, and medications for attention deficit hyperactivity disorder (ADHD). Taking these drugs may trigger a number of effects, including:

- Anxiety
- Risky actions
- Hallucinations (seeing things that aren't there)
- Delusions (believing things that aren't true)

EATING DISORDERS AND SELF-HARM

Eating disorders are a serious problem. They can lead to substance abuse and self-harm. If not treated, about 20 percent of people with eating disorders will die. Relationships also become strained. School and work are affected. Eating disorders involve:

- Binging: eating too much at a sitting
- Purging: getting rid of food by throwing up
- Starvation: not allowing the body to get enough energy by greatly limiting food intake

Studies show that from 25 to 65 percent of people who self-injure also live with eating disorders. Eating disorders and self-harm are unhealthy ways to cope with **trauma.** Trauma can cause our bodies to go through a process, or set of steps, like this one:

Releasing trauma in healthy ways allows people to heal over time. Repressing, or holding back, the trauma results in harmful behaviors, or actions.

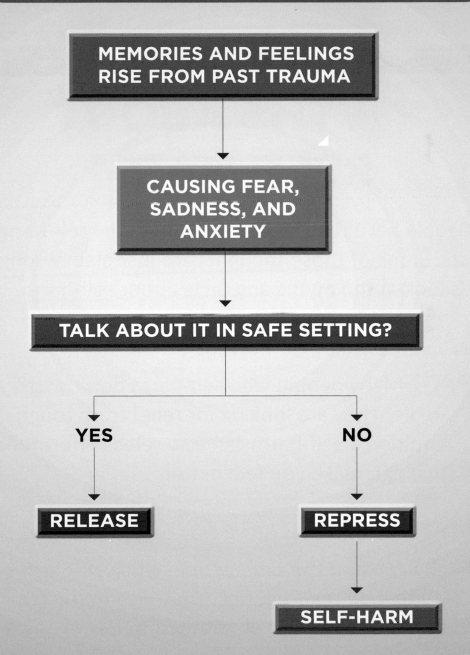

MEMORIES AND FEELINGS RISE FROM PAST TRAUMA

CAUSING FEAR, SADNESS, AND ANXIETY

TALK ABOUT IT IN SAFE SETTING?

YES

NO

RELEASE

REPRESS

SELF-HARM

MYTHS ABOUT SELF-HARM

People have many thoughts about why self-harm exists. Some of those thoughts are just plain wrong! Let's look at the myths and facts about self-harm.

MYTH Self-harm is a suicide attempt.

FACT Many people who self-harm don't wish to die. They are looking for relief from tough emotions. Self-harm can also release **hormones** that can make you feel better.

MYTH Self-harm is just a way to get attention.

FACT Most of the time people who self-harm try to hide their injuries. They also don't usually tell anyone about their behavior.

MYTH People who self-harm are crazy.

FACT Not everyone who injures themselves has a mental health problem. Even if they do, by calling people crazy, the **stigma** of mental illness persists, or continues.

MYTH Self-harming is just a "phase." Ignore it and it will go away.

FACT Some people may stop self-harming without help. But other people may not. People who self-harm are in pain, and they may not understand what is causing the pain, or how to stop it in a healthy way.

Happy, healthy people don't usually self-harm. It's important to learn the facts about self-harm; don't just listen to myths about it.

ADDICTED TO SELF-HARM?

Self-harm does not cause an addiction like taking drugs or alcohol. But experts say it can make you think and feel like you need it. You may enter a pattern by cutting deeper and more often.

Self-harm can lead to cravings and periods of stopping the behavior, then starting it again. This cycle is similar to other addictions. Experts say that people who cut have a behavioral addiction, such as gambling. Symptoms are:

- Overly focusing on, or paying attention to, the behavior
- Thinking it fixes problems
- Continuing to cut even though it causes distress
- Feeling nervousness before cutting
- Feeling relief after cutting

Brain chemistry may explain self-harm. The brain's **dopamine** and **opioid** systems may be involved. Dopamine is a brain chemical. It helps us feel rewarded. The opioid system lowers stress and pain. However, self-harm then often leads to unpleasant feelings such as guilt and shame.

A craving, or a strong and sudden want for something, can cause us to do things we wouldn't do otherwise.

Chapter 3

Getting Help

I would rather have a busted lip than hurt feelings. When my mom and I fought I always ran afterward, as fast as I could. Once, I took my pocket knife and cut open my thigh. It hurt, but I held back my tears. Boys shouldn't cry.

When the football team had tryouts, I got on the team. I spent a lot of time running and practicing. The coach cared about us. I talked to him about my mom. It helped. I also started talking to a counselor who helped me talk to my mom. After a while, cutting wasn't that important.

Sports can be a healthy way to deal with the ups and downs of life. They also teach us teamwork and hard work.

WHAT'S NEXT?

Maybe you've decided it's time for you to get help for self-harm. What's next? Here are some steps that will help:

1. Find someone you trust. This might be a friend or a family member. Or it could be a teacher or counselor at school.

2. Write about how you began to self-harm. Include details about what you do and how it makes you feel. Writing will help you to order your thoughts.

3. Prepare yourself. The unknown is scary. Will the person you tell about your self-harm be kind? Will they understand? Or will they get angry and upset? You can't know for sure. But thinking about another's reactions ahead of time can help.

4. Tell your trusted person about your self-harm. It probably won't be easy. But it is necessary.

If you are a teen who tells a close friend, know that your friend must tell an adult. Your friend needs help supporting you. An adult is the best person to help them—and you too.

A friend might be the person you trust the most. Or it could be someone else. Take time to think about who that might be.

WHAT HAPPENS IN TREATMENT?

Once you reach out for help, a medical worker will recommend treatment. This will likely involve meeting with a counselor. Counselors are trained to help you with self-harm. Together, you may work on some of these areas:

MINDFULNESS—This is a thought practice that involves focusing on the present without judgement.

DISTRESS TOLERANCE—This means learning to cope with difficulties, or problems. This practice shows you how to ride out bad emotions. It also helps you manage discomfort.

EMOTION REGULATION—This means having control of your emotions. This practice helps you to cope with bad moods. It shows you how to distract yourself.

INTERPERSONAL EFFECTIVENESS—This means improving your relationships with others. This practice helps you to communicate, or express yourself, better with others. This can cut down on conflicts.

MOTIVATIONAL INTERVIEWING—This means finding motivation, or a reason to act, to make a positive change. This practice helps you to think clearer. You can then decide whether or not to continue with self-harm in the moment.

There is no set amount for how many visits you need with a counselor. It depends on your own issues. It also depends on whether or not you cooperate. It's best to be open-minded when in therapy.

Counseling sessions, or meetings, may take place one on one or in small groups.

Chapter 4

COPING ON YOUR OWN

Recovery from self-harm often involves a lot of effort. Whether or not you are in therapy, you can do things to help yourself. Rather than cutting, there are other ways to distract yourself from strong emotions. Why not give some a try?

- Release anger by hitting a pillow. Stomp the ground. Flatten soda cans. Tear paper.
- Reduce tension through physical activities, such as running or boxing. You can even try yoga.
- Help ease sadness by chatting with a friend. Listen to a favorite song. Eat comfort food. Write about your feelings.
- Feel less numb by taking a physical action. An example is to briefly put your hand in ice water. Snap a rubber band on your wrist. Or clap your hands hard.

Learn to meditate. Turn your thoughts to your body. Shut your eyes and tell the muscles in your scalp to relax. Then your neck. Now your shoulders. Travel down your whole body this way while breathing slowly and deeply.

Movement can help when emotions overwhelm you. Being outside and away from your phone can also make you feel good.

OTHER WAYS TO COPE

There are a lot of other ways to handle tough emotions. The important thing is to remember that you have options. Calling or texting a helpline, such as YouthLine (text "teen2teen" to 839863 or call 1-877-968-8491) can be a good choice. The people who work for helplines are trained to help. Other options:

- Use the 15-minute rule. When the need to self-harm comes on, stop. Set a timer for 15 minutes and practice deep breathing (see page 39), meditating, or journaling. You will be proud of yourself if you can hold off.

- Learn to ride the wave. Urges, or strong emotions and needs, start out, then become stronger. If you resist, the urge will soon decrease, just like a wave.

Think about the times you have resisted an urge to self-harm. Jot them down in a notebook. Everyone has at least *one time* when they felt an urge but did not act on it. Look over the log to remind yourself of your successes.

Helpful Resource

The website Self-Injury Outreach and Support (*sioutreach.org*) has a lot of great information. It has true stories from people who have self-harmed. It also has info guides and ideas on coping.

Writing can be a powerful tool to resist self-harm. This is because it allows you to explore and unload your strong feelings.

DAILY ACTIVITIES

It's not enough to find ways to fight self-harm when the urge hits. Set yourself up for success. Use different strategies, or plans, to build yourself up, and do them every day. In this way, you will become stronger over time. After all, you have a whole life to live.

Our breath is with us at every moment. Focusing on your breath while relaxing is a powerful tool when battling self-harm.

Deep Breathing

Using breathing exercises can help a lot to calm yourself. First, find a quiet place where you can be alone. Put your hands on your belly. Draw air in slowly through your nose. Slowly, breathe out through your mouth. Repeat. Follow a count: breathe in for one, two, three, four; breathe out for one, two, three, four. Focus only on your breathing and feel your belly rise and fall.

JUST *breathe*

HEALTHY STRATEGIES

- Use breathing exercises.

- Keep a journal. Learn to look for things to be thankful for. There is always something. Even the fact that you can take a breath.

- Find a creative outlet. Sing, draw, sculpt, play music, or write stories.

- Pet a dog or cat. Walk dogs at an animal shelter or help clean cages.

- Spend time in nature. Being out in the sunlight helps raise your mood. Combine this with walking or playing a sport for an extra boost.

STRESS MANAGEMENT

Being aware of our levels of stress helps us know whether we're in danger of relapse, or falling back into negative habits. Ask yourself:

- Am I irritable, or easily upset?
- Do I get upset over small things?
- Am I feeling alone? Do I withdraw from others?
- Am I feeling worthless?

Our bodies hold stress too. Ask yourself if you are bothered by:

- Lack of sleep?
- Not eating? Or eating too much?
- Breathing problems?
- Fatigue (tiredness)?
- Lack of concentration, or the ability to think clearly?

Is your answer yes to one or more of these? Then take action by:

- Relaxing. Take a walk. Read a book. Play a video game.
- Eating healthy
- Getting exercise
- Sleeping enough
- Identifying goals
- Managing time
- Doing one thing at a time

If the source of your stress is a conflict, don't ignore it. Deal with the problem so that you won't be tempted to self-harm. The more you work at solving conflicts, the better you get at it.

Don't underestimate the importance of quality sleep. Being well-rested can better help you deal with stress and anxiety.

Chapter 5

HOW TO HELP A FRIEND OR LOVED ONE

If you think a friend is self-injuring, there's a lot you can do. First, remember, for your friend, it's not always easy to deal with tough issues. In fact, you may be met with anger at first. It's important to remain calm. Consider the following advice:

TALK ABOUT IT. Let your loved one know that you are there to listen.

ASK QUESTIONS. Show "respectful curiosity." For example, "How does self-harm make you feel better?" Be sure to listen.

DON'T JUDGE. It's more important to listen and understand. Don't show **pity**. This can make people feel like they are being talked down to.

DON'T PROMISE TO KEEP SECRETS. This could put you in a bad position.

GET HELP. Suggest they talk to a trusted adult or medical professional.

If you don't know how to approach your friend, say: "I'm concerned. I've seen scars on your body. If you are hurting yourself, you can talk to me about it. We can find someone else for you to talk to if you would rather."

Showing that you care is more important than the words you use. It's also important to remember your own health while caring for others.

Having one-on-one conversations can be hard sometimes. But it's necessary to learn to communicate with each other. Practice using "I" statements ("I am worried about you") rather than "you" statements ("You just need to stop cutting").

How It Ends

I left home for college when I was 18. It was hard to be away from home, and I cut my arms all the time. I couldn't seem to stop.

My roommate Ally was my only friend. We talked a lot.

One day, she closed the dorm room door. "I know that you cut," she told me.

"I don't—" I started to lie.

But she just rolled up her sleeve. Old scars ran across her wrists. "I got better. You can too."

"I don't think so," I admitted. "I haven't told anyone."

"You can talk to me about it," Ally said. "Or would you like to talk with the counselor who helped me?"

I thought for a moment. I'd seen counselors in social media videos and it seemed like they were helping a lot of people.

I took a breath. "Sure," I said.

GLOSSARY

aggressive: Acting with forceful energy and determination.

alcohol: A clear liquid that has a strong smell and can make a person drunk.

anxiety: Fear or nervousness about what might happen. Anxious means experiencing unease and nervousness, often about something that hasn't happened yet.

ashamed: Feeling guilt, shame, or disgrace.

bipolar disorder: An illness in which a person experiences periods of strong excitement and happiness followed by periods of sadness and depression.

conflict: A struggle between different forces.

deliberate: Resulting from careful and thorough thought.

depressed: Feeling sad, or affected by the serious mental health condition depression.

dopamine: A compound in the body that helps the nervous system send messages throughout the body.

emotional: Causing a person to feel emotion. Emotions are feelings, such as sadness, happiness, anger, and so on.

express: To communicate what you are thinking or feeling.

fentanyl: A strong drug used to treat bad pain.

frustration: A feeling of annoyance or anger from being unable to take a particular action.

hormone: A natural substance in the body that controls the way the body acts or grows.

intercourse: Sexual activity between two people.

LGBTQ: Acronym for lesbian, gay, bisexual, transgender, and queer or questioning.